Collected Poems
and
Susy Songs

Janet Elizabeth Stevens

Contents

These poems were written over the years of a long life. They encompass family, marriage, divorce, single parenting, and aging. This means they show joy, sorrow, grief, and determination, plus other qualities a person acquires in the course of a lifetime.

The Susysongs? My mother-in-law called me Susy sometimes. She liked the little rhymes, so Susysongs they came to be.

Every reader will not like every poem. Still, I think that every poem will reach out to some reader. Ideas travel through time, and fifty years from now, someone may pick up this book and find companionship in it.

May joy be yours,
Janet Elizabeth Stevens

PHILOSOPHY

The Road of Love

Love is not a flower growing
Upward from the mud and silt.
Love's a Roman road of living.
Love can't grow; it must be built.

Every stone laid with precision,
Each one fitting each before,
Firmly set on solid subsoil
Though the mason's hands grow sore.

Love is not a flower flaring
Briefly, for the world to see.
Love's a Roman road of living
Leading through Eternity.

Query

Lord—

        I do get most confused
        In trying to know:

What is prayer?
What is meditation?
What may conversion be?

        This bit I know
        Out of my living:

It is not only to think of Thee,
Lest my intellect distort my inner knowledge.

It is not only to feel toward Thee,
Lest emotion o'ersway my integrity.

        But it is to live,
        To be, for Thee.

Ceramics

Do not hide your feet of clay –
　See them, rather, so you may
　　Work the clay and pound it well,
　　Shape a sturdy pedestal.

In humility's sure heat,
　Bake with care, and then, complete,
　　Feet of clay, strange though it seem,
　　Can support a golden dream.

Size

I am quite aware
  Of the insignificance of my troubles
When I compare
  My moment with the cosmos.

Shall I then, meekly,
  Deny their importance to me?
And even more weakly
  Seek to erase them by comparison?

NO! I'M TRUE TOO!
Whatever has been, whatever will be,
I am here! I am now!
And I work, long, ache, hurt, and hope
NOW!

By contrast-
  Would it be less fair,
And perhaps gain comfort,
  To compare my worth
With the life of a microcosm?

Reward

Welcome the opportunity, then, of sacrifice.

No loss is it,
No deprivation,
No demand upon you,
No requirement.

Rejoice
To have this choice

of

Relinquishing the lesser
To let the greater be.

Do It!

If a whistle needs blowing,
Blow it!
If confusion needs sorting,
Sort it!

Wade in with wisdom,
Do what must be done.
You'll not be sorry,
Though it won't be fun.

You'll meet with opposition
As you work to set things right,
But you'll find friends beside you
To turn the darkness bright.

When the work's completed,
Look from where you stand.
Things are somewhat better
Because you took a hand.

Knowledge

For years I've known no fear.
The things that hurt me worst
Could not have been foreseen,
Nor sheltered from.

I hadn't known what I could stand,
And live, and find my life still good.

So now I walk free, walk unafraid,
To do and be what it is mine to be,
My purposes to fill.

I will not stain my time by fearing
What things may come about or what may be.
Enough, today, to joy in all about me.
No, no fear.

Parent

How can I teach my children patience
When I fail to curb my will?
How can I teach them perseverance
When I falter, stumbling, still?

How can I teach them faith and courage
When I know not where to turn?
How can I teach my children living,
I, who have so much to learn?

All

There has been pain.
I know the blessedness of its easing.

I know grief
And its passing, in time,
To a carried sorrow.

And I know joy
So deep and full and strong,
It carries all else on its surface
Like a sea.

After Anger

Shall I deny these truths my heart has spoken
    Because today they are no longer true?
Because today the bonds of bitterness have broken,
    And hope, and love, and courage flame anew?

Because today I've found new strength for living
    With what there is, not what I'd hoped there'd be.
Because today I've found new cause for giving
    Back to the world the courage given me.

Glance briefly, then, at yesterdays of sorrow.
    Today the world shines;
Fret not for tomorrow.

Required

There must be gentleness in me, for me to live,
Patience must be there, loving to give.

There must be space for loving, in all of the press,
And quiet contentment that never grows less.

Beyond all the turmoil, injustice and greed,
I shall know friendships, soul, spirit and seed
That saves for the future the Good that's to be,
So ages oncoming knows Good dares still be.

Youth and Age

We will never in our lives,
   Know as much as we did then.
Right was right and wrong was wrong,
   There was nothing in between.
There was no excuse, you see,
   For mistakes that "they" had made.
We could see their faults so clear,
   It made our own faults fade.
Proud we were, and right we were,
   Knew the way to go,
Never doubting of the path,
   Sure, so sure we know.

Now we know it's quite a job
   Just to keep our feet
Clean along the murky path,
   Bridge the gaps we meet.
Times we were the surest
   What lay on our way,
Proved to be a will-o-wisp
   Leading us astray.

Can't tell till we get there
   What's in store for us.
Put one foot before the last
   Without too much fuss.
DEATH? Another turning
   That we cannot see.
Friends have gone around the bend,
   Some day so shall we.

Will We?

It's easy to see what the other chap
　　Should do if you had the say,
So easy to blame another chap
　　For stumbling right into your way.
But oh, how hard to take time to lift
　　The stumbling block away.

If we could only live half as well
　　As we think our neighbors ought,
If we could do half the best we know
　　We'd reach the goals we've sought.
Love for man would be true, sincere,
　　And heaven to earth be brought.

I Had To...

So I got took.
No great surprise.
I can afford that sometimes.

Once in a while.

But just suppose
That I turned down a chance
To lend a hand for fear of being had,

And grown suspicious.

The lifting hand that might have healed and nurtured
And healed a heart
Had been denied.

How, then, could I have borne it?

Beverages

Tea you drink when feeling social,
In companionship of friends.
Coffee tops a brilliant dinner,
Brilliance to your evening lends.

When you're full of sad misgivings
And you feel you've missed your goal,
When you're feeling chilly, lonely,
Cocoa nourishes your soul.

Mine!

For almost every fault of mine
Heredity gets the blame.
And those it does not shelter
Environment can claim.

But when it comes to virtues,
I'll brook no loss, bereavement,
For every virtue I possess
Is quite my own achievement.

Hendrick Willem VanLoon

You set us properly in place,
    Minute, infinitesimal,
Of no account worth mentioning
    In history's processional.
However insignificant
    Our lives may seem to be,
One fact is undeniable,
    One worth is plain to see,
And mankind of the future,
    Their lucky stars should thank—
Without this generation,
    The future would be blank.

Compromise?

To settle differences 'tween friends,
A compromise is often vaunted.
Yet no one's happy in the end,
And neither gets the things he wanted.
Each one must sacrifice a part
Of some high vision he held dear,
And, in effect, he must deny
The truths that made him persevere.
So, rather vanquished would I be,
Could vanquishment not be prevented,
Than compromise and simply leave
Both parties always discontented.

So You're In a Rut?

So you're in a rut with walls so high
You can't see over the top,
And the drab, dull way ahead is long.
It seems it will never stop.

Right then, when your rut seems endless,
And you're worrying what to do,
Stick to your rut!
Remember: The fellow ahead got through!

You're Needed

Because I cannot cure the ageless problems,
Nor heal the heartaches of the total all,
There's no excuse for simply doing nothing
Nor any cause for shame at being small.

God made the universe, the world, and set it whirling,
And though the ancient wrongs are harsh and strong,
And every soul with any bit of spirit
Longs to strike out and rectify each wrong,

Do not forget. God also needs the small ones,
The little folks of life like you and me;
Though we're not shaped for world upheavals,
That does not mean we lack a destiny.

So don't burn out from anger and frustration,
Don't lose the low while reaching for the high;
You'll be stronger for the next thing that you try.

Just A Mirror

Which is mine in all my thinking,
Which is something I have read?
I seem most concerned with linking
Other's thoughts within my head.

So while I'm trying hard to be
The kind of person I'm supposed to,
I'm just reflecting constantly
The good and bad I've been exposed to.

Living

I cannot live forever on the peak.
The fierce breath-stealing winds of chance
Take from me even that thin air.

So look for me in the valley,
      Along the sunny south slope.
There I can till my fields,
      Watered with hope.
There I can feed my flocks,
      Pastured in love.

Yet always the avalanche
      Hanging above
Shivers my heart and soul,
      Shadows the sun.
Would God I were strong
      To command knife edged heights
Or could live resolutely with fear.

Which

In times of happiness should we
Be wrapped complete in joyousness?
Or should we hold aloof a bit,
Remembering unhappiness?

Would memories then make us wise
And help us guard ourselves from sorrow,
Or in remembering, would we
But taint with grief some bright tomorrow?

Going Ahead?

Shall I deny these truths my heart has spoken
   Because today they are no longer true?
Because today the bonds of bitterness have broken,
   And hope and love and courage flame anew?

Because today I've found new strength for living
   With what there is, not what I'd hoped there'd be?
Because today I've found new cause for giving
   Back to the world the courage given me?

Look bravely, then, at yesterdays of sorrow.
   Today the sun shines;
Gain strength for tomorrow.

FAITH

Service

Lord of the Cosmos, who has set
   Our little Universe in space,
Grant me contentment with my share,
   A satisfaction at my place.

In contemplation of Thy works,
   The endless whirling sphere on sphere,
May I not minimize the good
   That's found in lowly service here.

A sunny window, fresh and bright,
   A cupboard, orderly and clean,
A mended shirt, a smiling face,
   All add some grandeur to Thy scheme.

Eternity is long and deep,
   My life, infinitesimal power,
Yet may I not neglect to see
   The value of a well spent hour.

No Regrets

Should that gray curtain men call Death
Be drawn before my eyes tonight,
Have no regret, but picture me
As walking onward through the Light.
Although the future might not hold
Remembrance of this consciousness,
No future, even Death itself,
Can rob me of past happiness.

But should tomorrow hold, instead,
Anger and grief undreamed today,
Hopes unfulfilled, and goals ungained,
Life's bonds a barrier on my way,
Deny not what I've had of life!
The glance at glory I've been shown.
No gain, no loss can take away
The happiness that I have known.

Complete

Lord, Thou hast set me here in life,
Have given me my tasks to do.
I cannot understand Thy plan;
Enough that I am serving You.

Let me not wonder if there's need
For doing here this meager work,
Nor let me doubt Thy will, in greed,
Nor any humble duty shirk.

The time ill spent in searching out
The purpose of my being here
Might better far be used to make
A buoyant heart for someone dear.

When, with my Present I have joined
The future to the long ago,
Let me be done. With graciousness,
I pray Thee, Lord, to let me go.

Bible Class

"What is Truth?" the teacher questioned,
Saying he, himself was dumb
When it came to such a query.
Then he waited in the quiet for opinions sure to come.

"Truth is facts!" the answer quickly
Sped from lips of one so young,
Elders smiled; he'd solved world's problems
Ere his own had quite begun.

"Here's the Truth!" She raised her Bible,
Certain of her answer, sure,
For she'd found in it all answers,
Felt it kept her perfect, pure.

Most of us just sat and pondered.
If you'd asked us at the door,
Each one had the same idea.
Truth is what we're looking for.

At Hand

I thank Thee, Lord, that I can walk alone,
Without a need beyond Thy help to me.
That I can find with Thee my strength,
Nor weep too often in despondency.

Whole

God gave us heart and head and hands;
We need to use them all.
If we neglect to use some part,
We're pretty sure to fall.

So use your heart to dream the goal
That lies long years ahead.
And then, to choose the proper route,
You've got to use your head.

But still you can't expect to see
The things your dream is filled with,
If you forget to take account
God gave you hands to build with.

Laughter

Laugh and the world laughs with you;
Weep and you learn your friends.
Although the world will share a laugh
That's where its interest ends.

But a friend will share your sorrow,
For he's known sadness, too.
And he's learned what brings courage
To help you to live anew.

Laughter hides many faces,
But sorrow reveals, will confide,
Those who are willing to pull their share
And those who came for the ride.

Laughter you share with the whole wide world
And into the multitude blends;
So rejoice when your sadness finds comfort
In the hearts of a few wise friends.

Now Again

Now again comes the singing heart,
Now come the words to tell of life-full joy.
Working through to peace, comes the reward.

Now there can be
 Peace by achievement
 Peace by sustainment
 Peace by endurance
All of them good.

If there be pain
  I can absorb it.
If there be grief
  I can outlive it.
If there be sorrow
  I can endure;
Of that I am sure.

If there be grace
  I can accept it.

Not Enough

Being needed is fine.
　　　To bring my strengths, my skills,
　　　　　For the needs of those I love.
To add my bit toward balancing the scales
　　　That tip so heavily down.
　　　　　To be loved for my giving-
It is a big thing, to be needed.

　　　I wish I knew what it is
　　　Just to be wanted, as I am,
　　　Without any need to be met.

You, Too, God?

"Oh, it's fine to be needed,

To give My skills and strengths
    To care for those I love,
To reach into
    The crying, hungry, hurting of the world,
To tend My child with Love,
    To loose My talents out into the cosmos.

But times, twere sweeter far
    To be wanted, just wanted,
For who I am, for that I am,
    Wanted, cherished, not for what I do,
But just for being."

So, God, You, too, bog down at being needed,
Who meets our wants so full, abundantly,
And wish that we could turn, at times, in love,
Just wanting You
Who Are.

1946

When I shall die, no doubt I'll be
Buried with solemnity,
Flower decked and casket clad
Subservient to the current fad.

I, who know with wise delight
Earth's sweet surfaced loveliness,
Must be buried, concrete bound,
Left to mold to lonely dust.

How I'd rather blend with nature,
Be a part of earth and sky;
Oak tree, wheat field, fruit, or blossom,
Or a soft cloud, drifting by.

Custom, cruel art thou, and foolish,
Unblessed by necessity!
Why deny me room within
The cycle of fertility?

— — — — — —

1996—times change.
University Med school—then;
Ashes to feed the earth I love.

Acceptance

Quiet! 'Tis a house of grief,
A dream died last night.
Swiftly I must bury it,
The east is growing light.
None shall know its grave beneath
The mounting hills of duty,
None shall miss its presence,
None else knew its beauty.
The kettle hums a requiem,
I lay my dream to rest.
Heart, stop your grieving,
No doubt it's for the best.

Thanks For Being

Thank You, God, for making me
Part of such a wondrous world.

The glow in the west was changing
   Into the quiet of night.
Black clouds ranked to the southward,
   While the sky to the north was light.
High in the grayness a couple of stars
   Gave a hint of the Cosmos' might.

The wind in my face was frost tingled;
My heart rested in joy as I turned to the door.

Thank God, I am part of it all.

HOUSEHOLD

Sing A Song of Service

Sing a song of service, of humble duties done,
While a smile of happiness makes their doing fun.

Sing a song of service, of little children tended,
While tucked away in bureau drawers,
There's small sized clothing mended.

Sing a song of service, tending home hearth fires,
Never letting any know if your spirit tires.

Sing a song of service with gentle, loving word.
Let me by my serving life, learn Thy service, Lord.

Patches Speak

A patch denotes a certain thrift
  And wise economy.
What's more, it hangs your heart right out
  For anyone to see.

A patch that's firm and square and neat's
  The patch that always shows
A woman took her time and strength
  To mend her family's clothes.

So when a fella's overalls
  Are patched up neat and trim,
Be sure that there's a woman
  Thinks the world an' all of him.

Patching

"That's only a patchwork solution," he scorned.
"It's tacky, 'twon't last, not an hour." he warned.
But I went right ahead with the plan I had formed.

For I knew that a patch that was solidly set
Could take all the wear and the tear it would get.
That the britches once useless would sturdily do
Until there were means to replace them with new.

Any portion of life may require a patch.
When it does, set it gaily — if possible, match.
Don't scorn any makeshift that carries you through.
Give thanks, glory, honor, for they all are due.

At the Corner Box

Lord, bless these letters that I send,
And speed them on their way.
I want my friends to hear from me
Without the least delay.

This bill is due tomorrow;
I give you thanks indeed
For where-with-all to pay it all.
Deliver it with speed.

This letter carries yearning hopes
To set a matter right,
Where careless thoughts and hasty words
Have brought about a fight.

Please may the barrier that has come
Fall down at reading this,
That we may know again the trust
And love that may persist.

These two are for some loving friends;
I write as if they're here.
They understand my mind and heart,
For them, it will be clear.

They're on their way! I only hope
That what I wrote is wise.
Here's hoping, too, that one day soon,
I'll start to get replies.

No Apology

We need our Marthas in the field
Of poetry, as well as food.
Their ministry of simple thought
Is unassuming, yet it's good.

Eccentric poets frown thereon,
And would downgrade us if they could.
Our versifying is a craft,
May we enjoy it as we should.

Summer Dust

Sweep in the morning—
  Rolls of dust by afternoon.
Sweep at the noon time—
  Morning callers come.
Sweep during nap time
  Something's sure to interrupt.
Sweep in the evening—
  Day is almost done.

Tell me, when do you sweep
To keep your floors so nice?

What?! You really mean to say
You sweep your floors up twice?

January

Turn my work to the window's light,
Set the treadle whirring.
Turn of the year has come at last
And the cold keeps folks from stirring.

Rip and turn and patch and mend,
Snip, and stitch together.
There's sewing enough piled up to do
If the month should last forever.

Pajamas and shirts in an endless stream,
Aprons and dresses for me.
Ruffled curtains of springtime green,
A glorious sight to see.

Shriek then, winds! as you do your worst.
I shall not mind your blowing.
Here by the coal stove's ruddy glow
I can settle down to sewing.

Wait

The books will still be there to read,
The music there to hear,
The Art Museum's treasures
Grow richer year by year.

They'll wait for me, and be there still,
Beyond a timely door,
When comes the day I do not trip
On toys upon the floor.

They'll wait, untarnished by the years,
But there'll be no chance again
To help my little sons to be
Upright and goodly men.

These moments never will repeat
So I must use them now,
To teach them all the good I know,
The why, and where, and how.

Must answer all their questions,
Take time again, again,
And turn from contemplation
To the job of making men.

Responsible

There's always been dishes to see to
Or children to tuck into bed;
So I've never yet seen a whole sunrise
From starshine to golden and red.

Some morning in June I'll wake early,
And slip from my bed before dawn,
Then quietly glide through the hallway
And no one will know I am gone.

I'll go down to the end of the orchard
That's astir with the birds' restless song.
There, the sky is all open before me,
There'll be sunrise. It's where I belong.

As the gray turns to pearl edged with coral,
And the whole to a glow that's soul shaking
One part of my being will listen
To see if the baby is waking.

Contents

A pencil's full of magic, of poems, rhymes, and tunes.
It may contain a lullaby, or magic mystic runes,
A discontent, a hatred, a dream, a theme, a song,
An ache, a cry, betrayal, a lie, a truth, a wrong.

Consider, then, the pencils
 Ranged along the counter there —
Who knows what counsels they conceal,
 What triumphs, what despair.

For A Farm Writer

Many a good verse dies a-borning
If genius burns on a Saturday morning.
  For bread must be kneaded,
    The walls dusted down,
      The little folks' hair cut,
        A trip into town.

So what chance has verse
  To be given its wings,
When life is so full of
  More pertinent things?

Simple Living

Sing a song of simple living:
Books to read, and babies' glee;
Hearth fires burning in a cottage,
Kettle bubbling merrily.

Water fresh from hillside fountain,
Milk from Bossy, mild and meek,
Berries in the dew-touched meadows,
Waiting there for you to seek.

Tell me, where is Bossy stabled
When the winter blasts blow chill?
Who, then, cleans her dirty stable,
Carries water from the hill?

Wooden washtub, oh so cunning,
Smells of diapers, makes you retch.
Other stinks include a mouse nest
In the grassy cottage thatch.

Those who live their lives so simply
Bachelors be for wives don't care
Long to struggle in a cottage
Drying winter underwear.

Another Sign of Spring

Now, Husband, do you really think
Your muddy tracks don't show
Upon my fresh scrubbed kitchen floor
Since you walked in tip-toe?

It is a dear deception,
And I dare to laugh at you,
Who never never fool yourself
About what's really true.

You're sure if you looked closely
At the places where you stepped,
There'd never be a muddy track,
The floor would look well swept.

When April smiles between her tears
And crocus are in bud,
I find upon my kitchen floor
Your marks in April mud.

Take Off On Faust
(by a 1935 farmwife)

Should Mephistopheles rise from Hell
  Some winter washday morning,
And see me struggling with the fires,
  He'd pounce without a warning.

No life long love he'd offer me,
  To lure my soul away,
But running water, hot and cold,
  At any time of day.

Water enough to rinse three times,
  To feel the clothes are clean.
A big warm room to dry them in.
  That's tempting, what I mean.

Warm central heat that's free from dust,
  And easy on the fuel.
The coal and water that I haul
  Would wear out any mule.

To such a bounteous offer,
  Though his eyes with evil glisten,
On such a wet chill day as this,
  I rather think I'd listen.

PEOPLE

Manners

I knew a perfect lady,
When I was a little child,
And always in my memory,
I'll keep this story filed.

I went to visit her one day,
With Mama, to take tea,
And when she passed the cake,
She turned the biggest piece toward me.

Pregnant

A girl this child I carry?
   No, I hope it is a boy.
I don't feel I am fitted
   To teach a girl with joy
The things she ought to know.

How to set a room to rights
   And how to keep it so.
How to cook a meal and leave
   The pans and stove aglow.
How to plan her work
   So that sweet order will exist,
And free her from the pressure
   Of the cares that can persist.

Sequel

Oh, Timmie's come to our house,
A little bright eyed son,
And we are just as happy
As we were with the first one.
There's nails and there's a hammer,
A jar for toads that hop,
A Dad to teach him how to swim,
And a train to start and stop.
There's three kindly older brothers
To help when parents fail,
To tumble, tussle, roll and turn,
To make him boats to sail.

Oh Timmie, we're so glad you came
We needed you here, son.
And while the house seems full of men,
You're mother's shining sun.

Joyce

You are not less my sister, being dead.
The years that pass
Bring sisters into separate being
With separate family, friends, and interests.

But you, Joyce, being dead,
Remain the sister of my childhood,
A permanent relation.
The years can't change,
Or take away,
Or make us into strangers.

So we are always friends,
Though I am here
And you are now away.
Our laughter's that of children,
And there's nought
Can hurt our friendliness.

and yet —

Now the song is ended,
Now the dream is done.
Rest, dear sister,
Beneath a quiet sun.

E.S. and A.S.

Great chunks of wood fall from the saw,
As trunks of trees are cut.
The basement bins are heaping full.
Enough, then, is enough.

Yet all around the wood lot
The branches scattered stay,
Too small for the big furnace,
Too good to throw away.

The saw was loaded up again,
The truck went down the lane,
The branches cut to sixteen inch.
Careful there, take pain.

I saw them in my driveway,
And knew my friends had come
To bring me warmth for winter,
To cozy me at home.

My Franklin stove can use the wood,
But far more than that part,
The warmth they bring along with them,
With loving, warms my heart.

Underfoot

They're going to be in the kitchen,
They're going to play on the floor,
They're going to bring out their tractors,
Their trucks, and blocks by the score.

That is a little boy's privilege,
That is a little boy's right,
To play on a warm, snug kitchen floor,
Safe within Mother's sight.

I Have A Son

I had been lonely.
I had no one to walk over the fields with me.
There was no one with me to see
The leaf-cradled chrysalis blown by the wind,
The rain battered nest that was so lately home
To a now distant brood.
No one with me to watch the rain
Drop from the April willow leaves.

But now! Now I have a son to walk with me!
His nine year legs keep pace with mine,
His timeless heart keeps step with mine.
We shall explore the fence rows, find the trails
God's creatures have been making 'cross the farm,
Watch minnows in the dappled, curving creek.

Let other folks sit stagnant by the fire.
I have a son to cross the fields with me.

Need

I'm going to buy a hill some day
   That no one else shall know.
A little hill with a clump of woods
   And a twisting creek below.
A friendly hill, with a sunny slope,
   And a spot where wild flags blow.

I'll go to my hill for comfort,
   For a quiet time apart.
There'll be underbrush for a singing thrush
   And balm for an aching heart.

Secret

Love is not blind, dear,
Love knows quite well
All of your frailties.
Love does not tell.

Since love is kindly,
Sweeter than some,
Do not presume, dear,
That love is dumb.

Antithesis

My neighbor looks out from her window
As I swing along down the lane.
I know pretty well what she's thinking
As she peers through the shining pane.

"Whatever's she going down there for?
I wonder if anything's wrong.
Do s'pose that she's meeting somebody?
I'll notice if she is gone long."

The billowing clouds are above me,
The ground is still soft to my feet.
The glory of Maytime's round me,
The air is spring fragrant and sweet.

You can't explain blue to a blind man—
Why should I expect her to see
That I have a date with a red bird,
And a tryst with a willow tree?

My Pa

Now, some guys, when they fixes things
  'Eroun' the house fer Ma.
They gits their pliers an' a hunk
  O' balin' wire, an' la!
They thinks they's sot fer anything,
  From sewin' sheen t' screen door spring.
They doesn't know a thin', them dolts.
  But Pa, my Pa, he uses bolts.
A wire gouges at the wood,
  An' purty soon it chaws it thru,
An' 'nen you've got a fix-it job
  That's mighty tough fer you to do,
Er else the wire rusts out an' 'nen
  You've got the job t' do again.
But after all the rest's wore out,
  The fix my Pa has made still holts,
Cause Pa, my Pa, he even puts
  Sum washers underneath the bolts!

Timing

You've got to look at beauty
   When the beauty's there to see.
It may be inconvenient,
   But that's part of beauty's fee.

You've got to watch the brooklet
   Filled with wealth of spring time rain.
Summer heat will quickly dry it
   To a mudhole once again.

You've got to take your happiness
   Whenever it is found,
For there's not much left of sunset
   When once the sun's gone down.

Single

With wistful heart she said to me,
"Life has not passed you by."
Her gentle longing seemed to me
Like quiet April sky.

I answered softly, "No." And then
Unbidden thought my tranquil marred:
"But was it necessary
That it trample quite so hard?"

True

Jesus said, "Now, Mary, listen
   To my teachings while you can."

In the kitchen lonely Martha
   Struggled on with pot and pan.

Can't you hear the housewives whisper
   "Isn't that just like a man?"

Writer

Someone cared enough to write it,
   Felt he had some truth to say.
Someone found it worth the printing,
   Saving for another day.

With opinions of these people
   Standing always in my way,
Who do I think I am, then,
   To throw a book away?

I Cannot Be Sad—1945

Our Susy's been silent for quite a long time;
The cares of the autumn don't stimulate rhyme.
The coal must be ordered (they still haven't brought it),
The stove pipe put up (with persistence I fought it).
Yet through all this pressure, there's this thread of glee:
"I cannot be sad, for my lover loves me."

The yard must be raked of its summertime trash;
The rose bush be covered, it's tender and brash;
The carrots are dug, Oh how clinging the soil;
The squash carried up; Oh how tiring the toil;
Yet still through exhaustion this rapture I find
"I cannot be sad, my beloved is mine."

Essentials condensed to two warmable rooms,
For nearer and nearer the cold weather looms;
And we must be ready when cold weather hits,
To live in snug comfort as cozy as kits.
Yet the thought's ever with me, aglow in my heart,
"My beloved is mine, though we must be apart."

Young Son

Davy stood in his pajamas
Clean and pink and set for bed.
Then he started on the questions
Traipsing through his five year head.

"Is it morning time in China?
Are the children getting up?
Are they dressed and eating breakfast?
Has each got a Petey-pup?"

"Is the day as long as nighttime?"
So the conversation runs.
Then, impatient at day's ending,
"Couldn't God have made two suns?"

Release

Each wife, when blue, upset, distrait,
By heart of man or hand of fate,
Learns her own solace, how to gain
Courage to face the folks again.

One wife may buy a foolish hat,
Another, even now too fat,
Finds comfort at a soda bar,
While this one drives a speeding car.

This wife will lose her grief a while
In watching TV heroes smile.
Another reads, and finds her tears
Are one with women down the years.

But pen in hand, I'll force my grief
Into set words. I'll find relief
In shaping pain to measured words,
Bitter as wings of carrion birds.

Nettie

She stepped not on the violets;
In flower studded grass,
She waited quietly a while
To let a chipmunk pass.

Observant soul of beauty!
Courageous soul of love!
Teach me your strength to walk serene
The stony paths of love.

OUTDOORS

Joy

May I not serve, then, in Thy garden
And in Thy fields and farm,
Stirring the soil around the radishes
And pulling rhubarb by the fence?
Layering the Latham stems to make new growth
For warm sweet berries born two seasons hence?
Setting the tendril feet of runnered plantlets
In crumbled, tendered soil within the row?
Pausing to know the lilac's dearness,
The gentle petalled rose upon my lips,
The lemon balm so sweet on fingertips,
And the sharp, wild scent of catnip cornered there.
Or, tractor mounted, turn the vibrant earth
Warm to the sun in overlapping layers
Of joy and productivity.
At star shine,
Crimson clover in stretching, wilting rows,
Cut at first bloom to hold all good within.
Quiet in star glow for tomorrow's turning
To tomorrow's sun.

Perhaps

When April rains turn willows green,
   And bloodroot bells begin to blow,
The bluffs along the creek might be
   Illusion lifted from Corot.

Could I be quiet long enough,
   And watch unblinking, I might see
The circling dance of woodland nymphs
   Beneath a leafing maple tree.

Finding Out

Robin

The robin is a friendly bird,
   I see him in our tree.
His nest is full of sky blue eggs,
   all hid away from me.

Before a summer thunderstorm,
   he sings out sharp and clear.
He's high up in our maple tree
   and knows that rain is near.

Oriole

Shining and flashing
   way up in the sky,
I see a gold oriole
   winging on by.
His nest is a-swinging
   from maple top tip.
The nestlings come tumbling
   and land with a flip.

Meadowlark

By his bright yellow waistcoat
   with a shiny black V
You'll know it's the Meadowlark
   there that you see.

On a fencepost or wire
   he'll perch and he'll sing,
"Sit SEEEEER" he will whistle,
   hurray! Now it's Spring!

Chickadee

He flies to the feeder,
   and picks up one seed,
Then back to the bushes
   where safely he'll feed.
Black cap tells you clearly,
   the white stripes you see,
While his call tells you surely,
   he's a fine chickadee.

Nuthatch

Headfirst down the tree trunk,
   pausing on the way,
Picking bugs beneath the bark,
   food for him today.
He's a nuthatch, you can see,
   white breast and black back,
He'll be with you all the year,
   nothing will he lack.

House Finch

The daddy of this family
   spilled red jam all down his head,
Finch mama's striped feathers
   hide the babies in their bed.
Sunflower seeds they shell out,
   leaving just the hull,
Greedy little rascals,
   I can't keep the feeder full.

Scarlet Tanager

Sharpen your eyes
  in the hot summertime,
Search in the tree tops,
  for I'm hard to find.
I flit through the air
  on silent black wings,
And my body is red
  as the scarlet of kings.
I'm the tanager making
  my way to my nest,
High up in the tree tops,
  I find is the best.

Kingfisher

See him swooping from the sky,
  picking up a fish,
Flashing like the sky itself,
  blue as you could wish.
Feathered crown to make him king,
  fishing is his game,
From a high tree near the lake,
  kingfisher's his name.

Owl

Out in the night
   in the dark of the woods,
      An owl floats on velvety wings.

His "Hoo-oot" as he's hunting
   is not like the song
      That any bright summer bird sings.

I've heard that he's wise,
   and he looks very kind,
      As tame as a chickenyard fowl.

So when I am big,
   I'll go out in the dark
      And find me a friendly brown owl.

Threshing

As wagons loaded in with wheat do come,
All odorous with summer's harvest sweet,
(I could drown so contentedly in wheat.)
I take my cupped hands brim full,
Hold to my face for sound and sense and knowledge
Of its full berried being.

Best

There's rains that drench the violets,
   There's those that beat the heat,
There's those that send the city folk
   A-scurrying up the street.

Best of all the cheerful rainfalls
   That I have ever seen
Is that which comes in middle March
   And turns the wheatfields green.

Again

Once again the fields may know me, once again.
The lifting boughs bring courage to my soul;
The whipping wind that strips me of all—
I have been housebound now, for far too long,
Held by child bearing, limited by the loss
Of strength I gave my sons.

Now I may know the roughness of the tree trunks,
Rain on the willows, clover-sweet air.
Now I may feel the life-burdened earth against my breast.
Now I may know
The swift sweeping seasonal turn,
The four quartered cycle of time.

Fer Some

Fer some queer folks
   The robin is the surest sign of spring,
Fer some, it's pussy-willows,
   Fer some, a bluebird's wing.
Er else it may be violets,
   Er blossoms on the plum,
Er little frog a-peepin'.
   All these mean spring fer some.

But Winter's back is broken,
   An Spring hez set her stamp
When we kin eat our supper
   'Thout a-lighten' up the lamp.

Seventh Month

Evanescent as Christmas globes,
An instant here—an instant there.

The fireflies delight the dusk
and celebrate July.

Haying

Up on the rack on a hot summer day,
Head full of scent of the red clover hay,
"Gee up there Brownie" and " Get along, Bay."
All on a summertime morning.

There in the next field ripples the wheat,
Green at hay cutting, now ripe in the heat,
Ready to cut, to thresh, and to eat.
All on a summertime morning.

How smooth all the world looks from up on the rack,
Everything taut, not a tree-branch hangs slack.
Brilliance untarnished, sun warm on my back,
All on a summertime morning.

Everything shrinks to a size very fetching
Under a blue sky with clouds posed for catching,
All for the world like a copperplate etching,
All on a summertime morning.

Ultimately

A seedling stood in the woodsy brush
Leaves opening out to the sun,
To be blown by the breeze,
To soak up the rain,
To make of itself a tree.

Summer by summer,
Season by season,
Ever increasing,
Ever building,
Maturing,
Dying.

Then comes the woodsman
Cutting and hauling,
Bringing you to me.

Now in midwinter, here by the fire,
Releasing the sun warmth,
Flickering the sun light,
Smoke rising upward.
Gone, now, to ashes.

Thank you for being.

Harvest

"Except a grain of wheat shall die" —
To me as well does this apply.
  When I'm worn out with well-doing,
  When ahead a storm is brewing,
  When demands on me are strong,
  And I find no day is long,
  For the work there is to do,
  When I pray for guidance, too.

Let me know my life is certain
As the wheat beneath snow's curtain
Let me question not, nor fear.
I shall grow. My Saviour's near.

I grow strong through inward pain
As wheat shoots up in April rain;
Dying daily, yet in growth
Finding a far richer worth.

When my harvest time's at hand
May I have enriched the land.
May my life be full, complete,
Equal to a head of wheat.

It's Fall

It's time to get the feeders out
  And brush off webs and dust,
To check the hangers on them,
  To touch up any rust.

The tube gets filled with sunflow'r seeds,
  The flat with bird seed mix;
Around the stump I spread some corn
  Where doves get in their licks.

First come the busy sparrows
  To sample every treat;
They send the word out "It's OK,
  It's safe for us to eat."

The chickadees are next to show,
  And you will see them hang
Quite upside down upon the branch.
  They make a cheerful gang.

Soon cardinals are coming
   And finches heading south.
A bluejay flies up in a tree,
   A peanut in his mouth.

A tricky squirrel will find a way
   To tip the feeder's rim.
We'll nail an ear of corn up high
   Especially for him.

The entertainment that you get
   Can nowhere else be found.
It's you who make it possible
   By the feast you've spread around.

The First Cicada

The first cicada shrilled tonight
And so I know by morn,
I can expect to find
Tossels on the corn.

"Six weeks till frost" some claim he sings;
Timid souls are they,
Who feel that autumn follows fast
On Freedom's holiday.

To me, he says, "It's summer now."
The time of rapid growth,
Of swelling pods upon the beans,
And threat of summer drouth,
Relieved by warm and soaking rains
To fill earth's questing mouth.

Hot nights when scarce a breath of air
Can filter through the trees
To make the whitened curtains flare;
Growing nights are these.

Best of all, I share in it,
Growing, swelling, too,
Giving of the best of me,
Building life anew.

Harvest time will come with fall,
Then the earth and I
Share increase together
Beneath October sky.

The first cicada shrilled tonight,
And so I know by morn,
I am almost sure to see
Tossels in the corn.

Delight

Dance in the wind, my heart.
My feet may lag, but you, you need not wait.
Dance in the wind and touch
The maple's lifting leaves.

Smile at the water's curl
In pebbly creek bed's turn;
Answer each sparked jest
With laughter of your own.

Gladly, then, Spirit, go!
Forgive this body's dearth,
Stay not for my human feet,
Oh be not bound to earth.

March

Next month is April
With violets blooming
There on the South side
Sweet in the grass.

Next month is April
With robins returning.
Next month is April,
And this month will pass.

SUSY SONGS

I, who would write a love song
To last throughout all times,
Find myself entangled with
These pesky little rhymes.

Home

When I begin to sweep the floor
To make the room look nice,
The marbles run before the broom
Like multicolored mice.

Organize!

It's not that I dislike my work,
Indeed, I dearly love it.
But I must register complaint:
There's simply too much of it.

Once Upon A Time

A Mother Goose Queen lives an excellent life,
For honey flows from a fount.
There's a laundry maid to hang out the clothes,
And the King has money to count.

Yes Indeed

The Marys get the headlines,
Cheers, and flags unfurled.
I'd like some recognition
Of the Marthas of the world.

My Choice

My system of spending is faulty,
My house has a threadbare look.
But I have yet to see an occasional chair
Bring as much joy to me as a book.

Don't Snitch

I think it must be nice to be
The kind of soul who's able
To keep a jar of candy
Sitting on the table.

Mutual Flaws

Women are frivolous, foolish and fickle,
Never content at the work that they do?
I'll gladly accept your charge, Husband,
But tell me now, truly, aren't men like that too?

Do You?

This advice will make you rich
If you will only heed it.
Pause before you buy a thing,
"Do I really need it?"

A Form of Loving

I never see a patch that's set
In some big farmer's britches,
But what I see a woman's hand
Setting patient stitches.

Dear One

As April rains bring dandelions
Into sudden bloom,
So my heart's aglow with glory
When you step into the room.

Beloved

A happy sight you'll not forget
Nor are you apt to miss:
The smile upon a woman's lips,
Remembering a kiss.

Fulfilled

Give Sweet Sixteen her innocence,
And Twenty Two her charms.
I feel my most enchanting
With my baby in my arms.

Martha, Too

While Mary sat at Jesus' feet
Accordin' to his wishes,
His Maw wuz in the lean-to
A-helpin' with the dishes.

Living and Learning

We do not like the headaches
Nor the heartaches we must face,
But at least we learn compassion
For this aching human race.

The Work's Done

Lord, when I've dried the last clean plate
And laid it on the pile,
Before you give another life,
Please, can't I rest a while?

Reincarnate?

I need another life to live,
If God would only give it,
For when I've made the living,
There's no time left to live it.

Where?

A poet needs quietness if she's to find
A rhyme for a phrase that is fresh in her mind.
Our gay little rascals defeat thought and mood.
Ideas aren't missing, but oh solitude!

Fruit

I would be like an apple tree,
Mindful of my duty.
And like it, too, I would combine
Usefulness with beauty.

Private Battle

One secret I have learned that keeps
My versifying fun:
Never write about a problem
Until the struggle's won.

Call for the Oil Can

Quiet patience is a virtue
And I pray mine be increased.
Yet I can't forget the adage:
"It's the squeaking wheel gets greased."

Restrain

When angry words fly to your tongue,
And angry thoughts your mind have fretted,
Bitterness, when unexpressed,
Is then the least regretted.

Another Land

No day seems to be quite completed
Despite the full life that I lead,
If I don't have a few quiet moments
In which, with clear conscience, to read.

Age with Joy

Why strive for youth so ceaselessly
Or feel it's a disgrace
When wisdom garnered through the years
Is reflected in your face?

Dull

Saddest are those who do not claim
The wisdom they have earned.
When, even though they've struggled,
They never seemed to learn.

Differ

I can't expect another
To take the path I've trod.
Each must clear his own way
Up the hill to God.

Insight

Too quick we count another's faults
And find they make a tidy sum.
Let's cultivate a heart that sees
Temptations they have overcome.

Sure Would

There's instructions in full self expression
And methods to lay bare your soul.
But I'd like a sure-fire system
To teach me complete self control.

Keep On The Path

Perfection seems so far from me
I often feel like crying.
Though I may never reach it,
I'll never give up trying.

Outcome

When I have a quarrel with my neighbor,
I don't rave or rant, shriek or curse.
There's revenge that is sweeter by far unto me:
I go home and put her in a verse.

Don't

Avoid ultimatums
When you are provoked.
All too often
They have to be revoked.

Strength Gained

I don't go to church 'cause I'm better than you,
Or to make a big show, looking meek.
I go for the spiritual help I must have
To be strong for another long week.

Friendly

Don't do to others as you would
That they should do to you,
But with an understanding heart,
Do what you think they'd like you to.

Alone

I'll not deny my muse her grief because my Love
Dislikes her company unless she smile.
I shall not make her grimace shamefully,
But wait with her in solitude a while.

Just Me

I've memorized courageous songs
And practice diligently at them.
They comfort not, because I find
In life, as well as song, I flat them.

Must You?

I know that I am full of faults,
Admit they are terrific.
Yet something in me bristles up
When you make them specific.

Sunshine

Picnics bore you silly,
As my loving eye can see,
So I will raise some children
To go picnicing with me.

Can You?

If you would keep yourself well liked,
While seeming rather bold,
Don't disagree with people,
But opinions that they hold.

Don't Invade

So victory can't be achieved
Without a struggle or a ruction?
I think we could attain it by
A loving reconstruction.

So?

In every argument with him,
I'm always sure to find
My virtues I've learned from my husband,
While my faults are purely mine.

Hush

You think I'm being sulky
And ought to be hung.
It's just I'm keeping still until
I can control my tongue.

Grow

We pray every day for more courage
For patience, and wisdom, and strength.
But we're apt to resent all the trials it takes
To develop these virtues at length.

I Do, Too

My motto's faulty, yet withal,
My heart sings:
"Prayer changes me
And I change things."

Aunt Lucy

A mother's emotion is sung of
In lyric, in ode, and in chant.
But who can surpass the devotion
Of a gentle-faced sweet maiden aunt?

Value Your Work

This handmade look I try so hard
From sewing to erase,
I'd pay an awful price for
In some swell shopping place.

Of Course

'Tis the last of my earnest intentions
To steal thoughts or to plagiarize,
But it surely can't be considered a fault
That my mind is in tune with the wise.

I Hope So

The stars are all around me,
Their glory shines so near.
I feel so insignificant.
Do you think God knows I'm here?

Enough

My candle sheds a steady glow;
It seldom burns up bright.
But it is long and strong enough
To serve me all the night.

Lucy

She was a gentle, kindly soul,
Ill temper ever quelling.
When met with disappointment,
She sighed, instead of yelling.

Mutual

A poet should be universal,
Write for more than the well chosen few,
So his reader will feel, upon reading his verse,
"Why, that's how I think of it, too."

Estimate The Strength

The bridges you might have to cross,
Inspect with greatest care.
Although you may not need them,
You'll know the load they'll bear.

Yes

I break my budget all to bits
And then attempt to mend it
By this old true and timeworn phrase:
"There's lots worse ways to spend it."

Just Me

I do not like reproof.
It's difficult to heed it.
But still I can't deny the fact
I all too often need it.

Empty

I do not think that love can change to Hatred,
Assume an unknown heart, and ugly face.
No, when a noisy quarrel sends Love far fleeing,
Hate slinks in, assumes Love's empty place.

Parenting

A bit of child philosophy
A thoughtful parent learns:
Respect can't be demanded—
It always must be earned.

Fulfillment

I thank Thee, Lord, that I can walk alone,
Without a need beyond Thy help to me.
That I can find myself with Thee my strength,
Nor weep, too often, in despondency.

Distance

How can little children know
Emotional security,
When all too often, they are only
Guests till their maturity.

Sorrow

It isn't the high flying fancies of youth
Whose failures have made me abject.
It's the small disappointments of brave little plans
I had felt it was safe to expect.

So Do It

You will never hear me saying
"I've got more than I can do."
That is just a plain admission
I have bit and cannot chew.

Look Inside

Don't value a book by its binding.
You're quite apt to make a mistake,
For some of my favorite friends, like my books,
A drab first appearance do make.

Use Your Time

When you're feeling sad and gloomy,
And no job seems worth its pay,
Finish up the work you started
On some brilliant yesterday.

Release

Hold back your heart and regard it with care,
Keep it protected from friction and wear,
Never exhausted by rapturous giving,
Never disheartened—but never half living.

Look With Love

Too quick we count another's faults
And find they make a tidy sum.
Let's cultivate a heart that sees
Temptations they have overcome.

But I Can't

No doubt you like me as I am
but you could never raise objections
If I could keep my virtues
And dispense with all my imperfections.

Keep It Simple

Order is a cheerful thing,
Contentment ever giving.
It takes care of necessitities
And sets you free for living.

Sign of Fall

The first cicada shrilled tonight
And so I know by morn,
I can expect to find
Tossels on the corn.

Youth

It's fun to cut a swath so wide
That folks can see it plain,
But are you smart enough to make
Your hay before the rain?

Enrich

Living can be most exciting,
Life is whatever you make it,
So choose all your books with the greatest of care,
Let your reading enhance, not escape it.

Imperfect

I pride myself on tolerance,
Yet with a heart that's sinking,
Admit intolerance of those
Biased in their thinking.

Human

You are a farmer, you will always see
Weeds in every garden, every flaw in me.
Yes, I know my failures are desperately true;
But can't you believe, dear, Beauty's true, too?

Driven Out

These words reflect an attitude
That bids a husband roam,
When wife says, "This is my house."
Instead of "Here's our home."

Prayer

Greatest of all the gifts Thou has it
In Thy power to impart,
Greater then courage, grace, or wisdom,
I beg an understanding heart.

Misunderstood

The world expects church goers
To be supremely good,
The fact we go because we're bad
Is not quite understood.

Questioning

Love will sometimes winter-kill, losing all its shoots
But it's always sure to start up from the roots.

I never worry that Love might be lost,
But sometimes I wonder can it stand the frost?

Look At Yourself

Oh this divides the world into
A bunch of fighting factions.
We judge ourselves by our ideals
And others by their actions.

You Bet

No problem can discourage me
And don't you ever doubt it,
As long as I've got what it takes
To write a verse about it.

Womanly

A sound philosophy is worthy
Of attention men may give it.
There is this difference: while the men
Expound at length—the women live it.

Although to every worthy cause
I am no great persuader,
I'm doomed to finish out my life
"Perpetual Crusader."